A special book for

Stella Stainless and Cybil Marie Silver

Cousins and Friends Forever

Acknowledgements

Published by
Prairie Street Art
www.prairiestreetart.com

ISBN 978-0-692-8677-1
Copyright © 2017
Written by Ron Nelson
Illustrations by Marge Othrow
Book design by Ron Nelson

Dedication

This book is dedicated to my dear wife-
Adrienne.

Adrienne was the proud Mother of 5 Children
and Grandmother to 9.
Adrienne loved children.
Not just Family, but any little one
she got to know. Never a harsh word.
Her guidance and caring is
remembered fondly by all who knew her.

Good morning. I'm Stella, fresh from the shower and I am ready for another busy day.

A quick cup of coffee...

**And then feed
the Baby!**

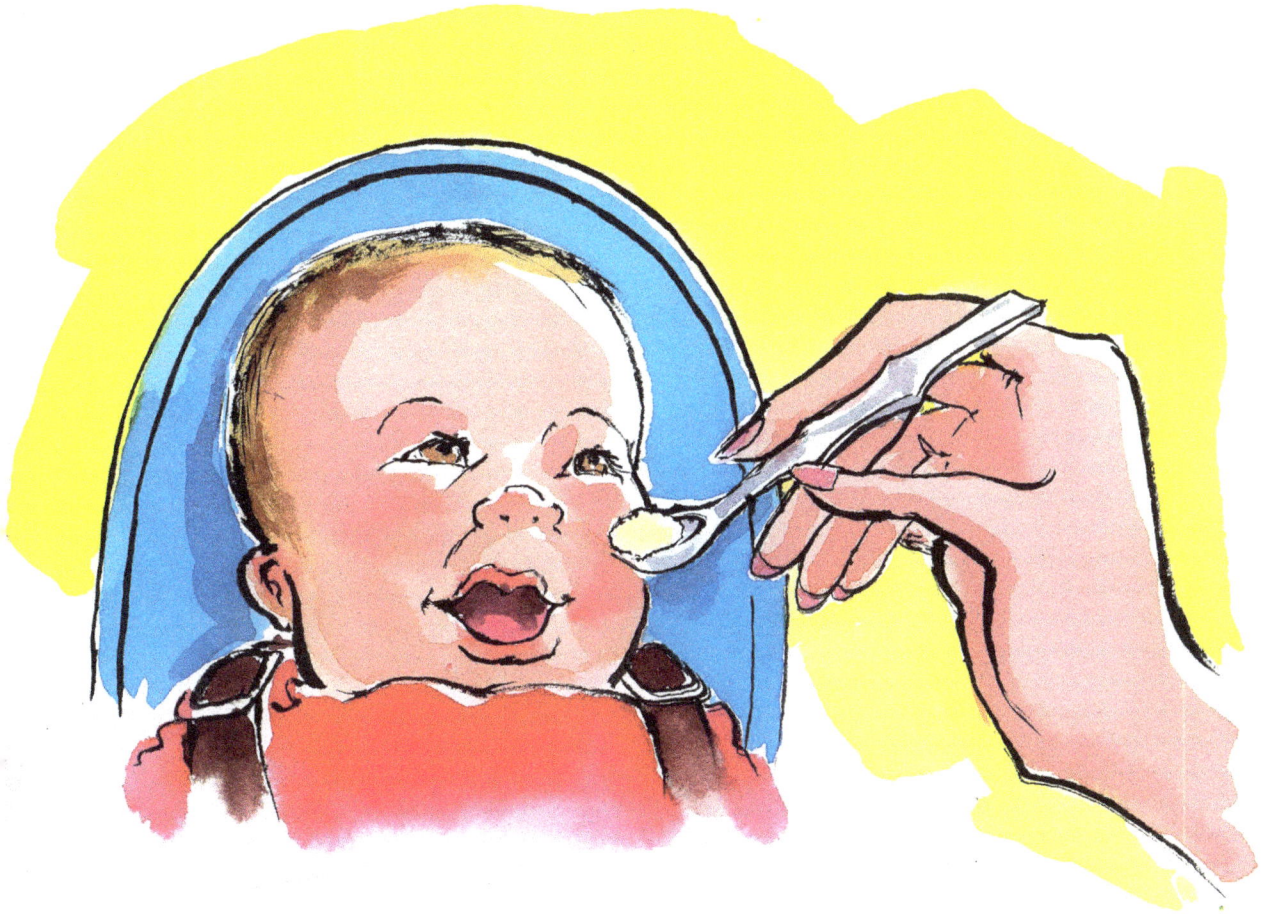

Sometimes I'm used as a tool

or to scoop out the cat food!

Some times I'm dropped

or part of a joke.

Sometimes I get to go on a trip,

and that can be exhausting.

At times I wish I had

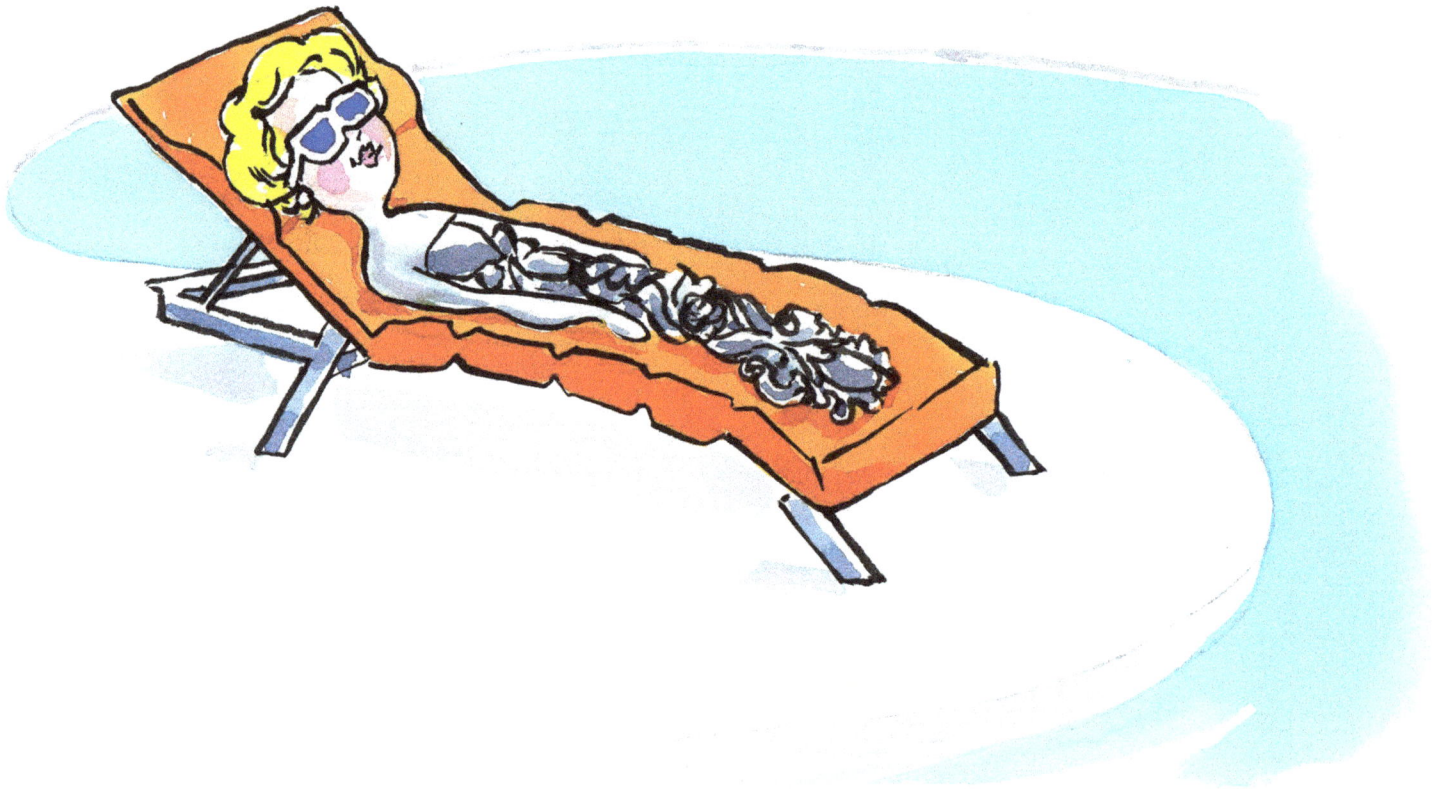

the easy life like Cybil

But, she knows that can be lonely.

Cybil only gets
called for
"Special Occasions"

She will do tea or desserts!

But, I love it when we are all

together on special occasions

Once after a party
I almost got put away
in the big silverware box.

They caught it
and it was back
to the drawer.

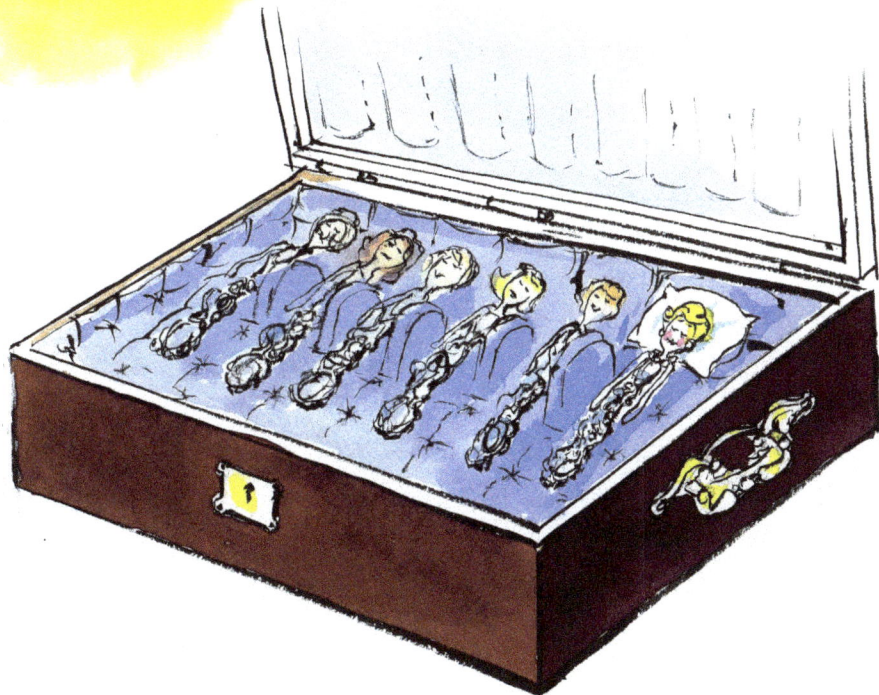

I like to know those who are different.
I like them and we all learn from each other.

Making new friends is important. You will enjoy their company and they will enjoy yours.

I know there are times when Cybil is lonely.
Sometimes it is months when she does nothing.
She counts on me as a friend and longs
for the companionship we have.

So, let's keep the joy and good times we have
during celebrations, the love we have
for each other.

Through good times and bad, the strength
and love of our friendships
last forever.

www.ingramcontent.com/pod-product-compliance
Lightning Source LLC
Chambersburg PA
CBHW060802150426
42813CB00059B/2850